Well Read 4

SKILLS AND STRATEGIES FOR READING

Instructor's Pack

Mindy Pasternak | Elisaveta Wrangell

OXFORD
UNIVERSITY PRESS

OXFORD
UNIVERSITY PRESS

198 Madison Avenue
New York, NY 10016 USA

Great Clarendon Street, Oxford OX2 6DP UK

Oxford University Press is a department of the University of Oxford.
It furthers the University's objective of excellence in research, scholarship,
and education by publishing worldwide in

Oxford New York

Auckland Cape Town Dar es Salaam Hong Kong Karachi
Kuala Lumpur Madrid Melbourne Mexico City Nairobi
New Delhi Shanghai Taipei Toronto

With offices in

Argentina Austria Brazil Chile Czech Republic France Greece
Guatemala Hungary Italy Japan Poland Portugal Singapore
South Korea Switzerland Thailand Turkey Ukraine Vietnam

OXFORD and OXFORD ENGLISH are registered trademarks of
Oxford University Press

Editorial Director: Sally Yagan
Senior Publishing Manager: Pietro Alongi
Head of Development and Project Editors: Karen Horton
Associate Development Editor: Olga Christopoulos
Design Director: Robert Carangelo
Design Project Manager: Maj-Britt Hagstead
Project Manager: Allison Harm
Production Manager: Shanta Persaud
Production Controller: Eve Wong

ISBN: 978 0 19 476113 0

Printed in Hong Kong.

10 9 8 7 6 5 4 3 2 1

Contents

PowerPoint® Teaching Tool

ExamView® Test Generator

Notes to the Teacher

Welcome to **Well Read**, a four-level series that teaches and reinforces crucial reading skills and vocabulary strategies step-by-step through a wide range of authentic texts that are meant to engage students' (and teachers') interest. **Well Read 4 Instructor's Pack** is intended for instructors using **Well Read 4** in their high-intermediate to low-advanced level classrooms. All of the texts in Well Read 4 are at the 11.0–12.0 Flesch-Kincaid Grade Level, and the student book contains 24–48 hours of instructional material, depending on how much in-class work is assigned.

In the **Well Read Instructor's Pack**, you will find two technological resources that will enhance your students' classroom experience: the **PowerPoint® Teaching Tool** and the **ExamView® Test Generator**. In addition, you will find the answer key to the student book.

PowerPoint® Teaching Tool

This data CD includes a set of fully-integrated PowerPoint® slides that serve as a valuable class management tool. These visual aids contain every activity of the student book except for the texts themselves, which students read in their books. The corresponding student book page numbers are always included in the bottom right portion of each slide.

The slides also contain all answers to text questions, and can be used as an answer key in class. The **Instructor's Pack** also indicates where each activity can be found on the PowerPoint® slides with an icon (⬚) that includes the slide number.

Given that the visual aids replicate, magnify, and provide color to the images in the text, they are intended to be used along with the student book to accommodate a **"heads up/heads down"** methodological approach with students looking both down at their books and up at the visual aids as directed by the instructor. For example, the texts are strictly a "heads down" activity, while reviewing the answers is "heads up."

Questions can have one of three types of answers: (1) no answer, usually because there are many possibilities, or it is a discussion question; (2) an answer or several possible answers; or (3) a click and type answer box in which the instructor can type an answer, several possible answers, a survey, etc.

Chapter Introduction with PowerPoint®

In each chapter of the student book, the opening page introduces the chapter's theme. The questions and photographs are designed to activate the students' prior knowledge, as well as stimulate some limited discussion before the previewing, reading, and post-reading activities.

⬚ The PowerPoint® slides contain the introduction page of the text over several slides. Students view this material with their books open or closed. Answers are provided at the click of the mouse.

GETTING STARTED WITH POWERPOINT®

This activity precedes each text or graphic component in the student book. It is designed to help students focus in on a more specific topic through reflection and discussion. It also introduces a small number of critical vocabulary words or phrases.

☐ The PowerPoint® slides can be used to present this activity or students can use their books initially and then the slides can be used for a classroom discussion of partner results. Answers are provided at the click of the mouse. Some questions have a box following them instead of an answer. On every slide that contains a box, **"click and type option"** is noted. Here, the instructor can enter answers elicited from students on the slides without pulling up the screen to write on the blackboard. To type in the box, click anywhere inside the box. The answers that are entered will remain until the PowerPoint® file is closed. They will remain permanently if the file is saved before closing, making it easy to see which activities have been covered in a given class. It is recommended that you save a copy and rename the file in order to retain a clean version of each chapter.

These **click and type** boxes are not only useful in order to type student responses, but they can also be used to try out and then erase possibilities. The backspace key works in the same way as with a word processor. Finally, the number of students who answered a question a certain way can be recorded in the boxes in survey format.

ACTIVE PREVIEWING WITH POWERPOINT®

Active Previewing asks students to read only brief and selected parts of the text, and then answer very simple questions that focus on this material. This activity encourages the notion that students do not have to understand each and every word of what they are reading. There is a strong emphasis on how to preview a wide range of genres, both academic and non-academic, including—but not limited to—newspaper articles, online texts, magazine articles, textbook articles, tables, charts, graphs, timelines, and graphics.

☐ The PowerPoint® slides can be used to get this activity started and to review the answers. For each set of questions, all the questions are shown first and then the answers come up one at a time. In this way, the entire activity can be done "heads up."

READING AND RECALLING WITH POWERPOINT®

The first reading activity asks students to read and recall. This is less daunting than being presented with an entire text, and also allows the students to retain more. Recalling encourages students to be accountable for the material they read. At its most basic, students build their short-term memories. On a deeper level, students begin to process information more quickly and holistically. Perfect recall is never the goal.

☐ The PowerPoint® slides contain the directions for this activity. The textbook is needed for the actual readings.

UNDERSTANDING THE TEXT WITH POWERPOINT®

After each text, students are presented with a two-part reading comprehension activity. The first part checks the students' comprehension of the most basic ideas expressed in the text, whereas the second part challenges the students to recall other key ideas and information.

☐ With the PowerPoint® slides for this activity, the text doesn't need to be opened at all.

READING SKILLS WITH POWERPOINT®

Among other essential reading skills, students are introduced to topic, main idea, and supporting details in separate chapters, which allows them to practice and master each of these skills before progressing to the next. Earlier chapters present choices in a multiple choice fashion, whereas subsequent chapters require the students to write their own interpretations. The ability to think critically about the information that is presented in the text is a crucial part of being an active reader. Students are first taught to distinguish between facts and opinions, and later, inferences. In the final chapters of the student book, students will be asked to find facts and opinions and to make inferences of their own.

☐ The PowerPoint® slides contain all the material from the **Reading Skills** boxes, so the instructor can take advantage of these slides to teach each reading skill.

VOCABULARY STRATEGIES WITH POWERPOINT®

Students first learn that they can understand the general idea of the text even without understanding every word; however, skipping words is not always an option, thus students are introduced to different strategies that can help them determine the meanings of new vocabulary without using their dictionaries. The various vocabulary strategies are presented and then reinforced in later chapters. All vocabulary activities present the vocabulary as it is used in the texts themselves, yet the vocabulary strategies that are taught can be applied universally to reading that the students do outside class. Developing these strategies will allow students to become more autonomous readers.

☐ The PowerPoint® slides contain all the material from the **Vocabulary Strategies** boxes and can be used to guide the class through the activities in this section. Both questions and answers are provided so this can be a "heads up" activity.

DISCUSSING THE ISSUES WITH POWERPOINT®

Every text ends with a series of questions that encourage the students to express their opinions and ideas about the general subject discussed in the text. The questions are designed to be communicative in that they strike upon compelling issues raised in the text.

☐ The PowerPoint® slides provide the questions from this discussion activity. The instructor can use these slides to remind students to keep on target.

PUTTING IT ON PAPER WITH POWERPOINT®

Reading and writing are two skills that inherently go together. The writing activity complements the chapter texts, yet it is also designed to stand independently should the instructor decide not to read all of the chapter texts. Each *Putting It On Paper* activity offers two writing prompts; the instructor can allow students to choose between the prompts or can select one prompt for all students to use.

☐ The PowerPoint® slides contain all the material from this section to facilitate discussion and review. Therefore this activity can be "heads up" to give students the directions and "heads down" to do the writing.

TAKING IT ONLINE WITH POWERPOINT®

Each *Taking It Online* activity guides the students through the steps necessary for conducting online research, based on the theme of the chapter. Instructors might opt to prescreen a select number of websites in advance, thus directing the students to more reliable and useful sites. *Taking It Online* finishes with a follow-up activity that enables the students to take their research one step further, in pairs or groups.

☐ The PowerPoint® slides contain the text material to support this section. A particularly valuable feature of the click and type option for this section is their use for entering Website addresses. Instructors can pre-select particularly worthwhile Websites to enter into these locations and the students can copy them. Alternatively, the file can be saved and that slide can be printed out and copied for dissemination. Given the complexity of some Web addresses, that can be a way to avoid errors and frustration.

ADDITIONAL TIPS FOR USING THE POWERPOINT® SLIDES

The use of the slides can foster an enjoyable, effective and efficient classroom experience. That they follow the textbook exactly means that the coordination between text activities and the visual aids is seamless. Instructors find that the use of this teaching tool facilitates many aspects of teaching, especially planning. This total class management tool takes the instructor and class step-by-step through each chapter.

In the best case scenario, a instructor would turn on the projector and keep it on throughout class and let the slides guide the way through each activity in the chapters. For the classroom in which the use of a projector is limited, one could use the slides to begin the chapter, for the **Understanding the Text** section and also to go over all answers. In either case, the ability to have students in the "heads up" mode can add a great deal to the dynamic in the classroom. The instructor can see the faces of the students and read their expressions for understanding or a lack of it. Students enjoy the beautiful art and photos and often pay more attention than they would with only a textbook.

If a computer/projection system is not available, overhead transparencies could be made to simulate the experience.

ExamView® Test Generator

This CD-ROM enables you to create customized reading skills tests for use with **Well Read 4**. You can use these tests

to assess student progress at any phase of the learning process: pre-test, chapter-by-chapter, or final exam. This tool will help you evaluate the effectiveness of your teaching, and it will allow your students to gauge their own progress based on their test results.

A large selection of questions in familiar question formats are featured on the CD-ROM: multiple choice, true/false, completion, and essay. The questions are always based on the skills and strategies covered in the corresponding student book chapter. In the **Banks** folder, there is a folder called **Well Read 4 OUP**, in which you will find **Question Banks** for each chapter of **Well Read 4**.

There are many ways to create tests using this CD-ROM:

Create a test in just minutes:
Use the *QuickTest Wizard* to select the type and number of questions you want to include from the question banks in the Banks folder.

Select specific questions:
Use the *Test Builder* to navigate your way through the question banks in the Banks folder, and pick specific questions to include on your test.

Write your own questions:
Create completely new tests using your own questions or edit the questions provided. In order for these questions to be available at a later time, they need to be added to the Bank file.

Important note: In *ExamView Assessment Suite®*, the reading passage is designed to appear with each different question type. For example, if you choose multiple choice, completion, and essay questions, the reading passage will appear three times. If you want the reading passage to appear only once at the beginning of each test, simply highlight and delete the other reading passages once you have finished creating your test.

All tests can be printed out for students to take at their desks. Test questions can be scrambled to appear in any order, multiple versions of a test can be created, and you can save all your tests on your computer to use for future classes. An answer key is automatically generated for each test you create.

Alternatively, tests may be administered by computer or online through a school website for an additional fee. The *ExamView®* website (www.examview.com) provides instructions for computer and online testing. You can also subscribe to the *ExamView®* Testing Center for access to a variety of services.

For easy, step-by-step instructions for using **Well Read 4 ExamView® Test Generator**, see the **Manual** on the CD-ROM.

Answer Key

2 SB p. 1 Chapter Introduction

2.

   a. Iraq

   b. the U.S.

   c. India

Text 1 Hollywood Dreams

5 SB p. 2 Getting Started

A.

   5. ticket sales, selling movie rights to television, soundtracks from movies

10 SB p. 3 Active Previewing

  Hollywood, movies, the movie industry

11 SB p. 6 Understanding the Text

A.

   c

B.

   1. b

   2. b

   3. a

   4. c

Text 2 A Movie Close to Home

18 SB p. 8 Active Previewing

  Jackie Oweis Sawiris, movies in Jordan

19 SB p. 9 Understanding the Text

A.

   1. c

   2. b

   3. b

B.

   1. Raz

   2. Jackie

   3. Jackie

   4. Jackie

   5. Raz

Text 3 At the Movies

24 SB p. 11 Active Previewing

   1. U.S. Motion Picture Overview

   2. b

26 SB p. 12 Scanning

   1. 2000

   2. $193,988

   3. 1995

   4. 26,995

   5. 2000

Text 4 Movies—Bollywood Style

32 SB p. 14 Active Previewing

C.

  Bollywood, movies in India, the Indian movie industry

34 SB p. 16 Understanding the Text

A.

   1. b

   2. a

   3. b

   4. c

   5. a

   6. c

B.

   1. Bollywood

   2. Hollywood

   3. Hollywood

   4. Bollywood

   5. Bollywood

Text 1 Online Dating

5 SB p. 22 Getting Started

B. Advantages may include: easy, can find people with similar interests, can meet people from around the world; Disadvantages may include: no common friends, distance from new friends, might not be safe.

6 SB p. 22 Active Previewing

C. dating, online dating

8 SB p. 24 Understanding the Text

A.

Do's: Spend time getting to know someone; give someone the chance to impress you; be happy; Dont's: Disclose too much personal information; tell little white lies; do all the talking.

B.

2. T
3. T
4. F You should always be honest online.
5. F It is important that you give the other person time to talk and that you listen attentively.

11 SB p. 25 Understanding the Topic

A.

a. G
b. S
c. T

B.

1.
   a. S
   b. T
   c. G
2.
   a. G
   b. S
   c. T
3.
   a. G
   b. T
   c. S

14 SB p. 27 Understanding Vocabulary in Context—Synonyms

2. to encourage
3. to overstate
4. to dominate
5. desire

Text 2 Love at First Smell

20 SB p. 28 Active Previewing

A.

1. Professor Tim Jacob
2. at Cardiff University or in the School of Biosciences or in Wales
3. that people choose their partners based on smell
4. when finding the perfect partner or when choosing a mate

C.

smell; choosing a partner

22 SB p. 30 Understanding the Text

A.

1. smell
2. different
3. their immuno-type or smell type or odor type

B.

1, 2, and 4

22 SB p. 30 Understanding the Topic

1.
   a. S
   b. T
   c. G

26 SB p. 32 Understanding Subject and Object Pronouns

1. Prof. Tim Jacob
2. smell
3. humans
4. sweat glands, apocrine glands
5. people
6. smell
7. a person
8. perfumes

27 SB p. 32 Understanding Vocabulary in Context—Synonyms

2. to guarantee
3. protection
4. basic
5. sweat glands

Text 3   The Best First Date

32 SB p. 33 Active Previewing

1. The Other Half: An E-Poll Dating Survey
2. What Women Think: The Ideal First Date and What Men Think: The Ideal First Date
3. the ideal first date; dating

33 SB p. 34 Scanning

2. 13%
3. going out for lunch or dinner
4. men
5. beach/park

Text 4   Close Friends

38 SB p. 35 Active Previewing

C. how proximity—or distance/closeness— affects relationships; meeting strangers; contact

40 SB p. 38 Understanding the Text

A.

1. when they live near each other
2. it makes them decrease
3. the one they saw most often (15 times)
4. it makes dating or marriage more likely or the closer people live to each other, the more likely they are to date or get married
5. because they are exposed to fewer people

B.

1, 3, and 8

42 SB p. 39 Understanding the Topic

A.

1.
   a. S
   b. G
   c. T

B.

1.
   a. G
   b. T
   c. S
2.
   a. S
   b. G
   c. T
3.
   a. T
   b. G
   c. S
4.
   a. T
   b. S
   c. G
5.
   a. T
   b. S
   c. G

45 SB p. 40 Understanding Subject and Object Pronouns

1.
   b. six billion people on the planet or people
   c. we the readers or we human beings
   d. two people
   e. two people

2.
   a. person
   b. we the readers or we human beings
   c. people

3.
   a. students (who are free to choose their own classroom seats)
   b. a student
   c. the student

46 SB p. 40 Understanding Vocabulary in Context—Synonyms

2. feelings or mood
3. shared
4. frequent contact with
5. nervousness
6. first

7. to increase
8. to control

CHAPTER 3   UNNATURAL RESOURCES

Text 1   Trash or Treasure

5 SB p. 44 Getting Started
3. garbage: a, c, e, f, h; to throw away: a, b, d

7 SB p. 44 Active Previewing
C.
1. waste, scrap, junk as an export to China
2. China buys junk/scrap/garbage from the U.S; The U.S. sells junk/scrap/garbage to China; There is a scrap trade between the U.S. and China.

9 SB p. 46 Understanding the Text
A.
1. because it was part of the junk the U.S. sells to China
2. the U.S. sells scrap/junk to China (OR China buys scrap junk from the U.S.)
3. China recycles the scrap to make other products/things.

B.
2. T
3. F The U.S. sells scrap to China.
4. F China has become the biggest customer for the U.S.'s junk.
5. T

12 SB p. 47 Understanding the Topic and Main Idea
A.
1.
   a. S
   b. G
   c. T
3.
   a. G
   b. S
   c. MI

B.
1.
   a. G
   b. T
   c. S
2.
   a. MI
   b. G
   c. S
3.
   a. T
   b. S
   c. G
4.
   a. G
   b. MI
   c. S
5.
   a. S
   b. T
   c. G
6.
   a. MI
   b. G
   c. S

17 SB p. 49 Understanding Vocabulary in Context—Phrasal Verbs
1. d
2. b
3. c
4. e
5. a

Text 2   Curb Appeal

20 SB p. 50 Getting Started
A.
4. a, b, c, and e

23 SB p. 51 Active Previewing
A.
1. curbside treasure hunters or people who collect others' discarded things
2. They collect other people's discarded things or trash.
3. on the side of the road
4. Saturdays or weekends

C.

1. curbside treasure hunters, people who collect others' throw-aways
2. Some people collect others' garbage because they think it's valuable; Curbside treasure hunters find valuable items in others' trash.

26 SB p. 53 Understanding the Text

A.

1. Luck, timing, weather, transportation
2. She uses them in her artwork and donates them to charities.
3. They help her save money or she's gotten a lot of things for her twins this way.

B.

a, d, e, g, and h

28 SB p. 54 Understanding the Topic and Main Idea

1.
   a. S
   b. T
   c. G
2.
   a. MI
   b. G
   c. S

30 SB p. 55 Understanding Vocabulary in Context

A.

1. mink, cashmere sweaters: expensive items or expensive clothes
2. stereos and TVs: items used for music, video
3. stereo components, vacuum cleaners, bicycles, a safe, and a typewriter: things that have been found

B.

1. c
2. c
3. a
4. b
5. b

Text 3 Simple Actions, Real Results

34 SB p. 56 Active Previewing

1. Simple Actions, Real Results
2. c, e
3. waste, waste reduction, reducing waste

35 SB p. 57 Scanning

1. Metric tons of carbon equivalent
2. GHG
3. 52
4. 1,569
5. 402
6. corrugated cardboard
7. preventing
8. recycling

Text 4 Building Tires

40 SB p. 59 Active Previewing

C.

1. tires, scrap tires, used tires, uses for old tires, research on scrap tires
2. There are many uses for scrap tires; There are a number of ways to use scrap tires.

42 SB p. 62 Understanding the Text

A.

1. a professor (emeritus) (at the University of Arizona)
2. to find solutions for an environmental problem
3. There are more and more of them, and they create environmental hazards / dangers.
4. dams, houses, fencing, bullet stops, bridge supports, playgrounds, freeways, storage structures, fuel, general engineering projects
5. They are convinced they are useful as dams or they like them.

B.

1. Use: to line lawns / grass
   Advantage: to save water
2. Use: engineering / construction
   Advantage: costs less
3. Use: as bedding for livestock
   Advantage: allows liquid to drain

4. Use: house construction
   Advantage: easy installation; tires are free
5. Use: retaining walls/dams
   Advantage: reduces damage of flooding; costs less

<u>44</u> SB p. 62 Understanding the Topic and Main Idea

A.
1.
    a. S
    b. G
    c. T
2.
    a. MI
    b. S
    c. G

B.
1.
    a. S
    b. T
    c. G
2.
    a. MI
    b. G
    c. S
3.
    a. G
    b. T
    c. S
4.
    a. S
    b. MI
    c. G
5.
    a. S
    b. G
    c. T
6.
    a. S
    b. G
    c. MI

<u>48</u> SB p. 64 Understanding Vocabulary in Context

A.
2. concrete, steel, wood: material/things we normally use for building

3. cows, sheep: farm animals
4. food scraps, grass cuttings, leaves, paper: natural materials

B.
1. d
2. f
3. e
4. a
5. b
6. c

CHAPTER 4   UNCOVERING HISTORY

<u>3</u> SB p. 67 Chapter Introduction
2.
    a. pre-Aztec city of Teotihuacán, Mexico
    b. Egypt sphinx
    c. Mayan stone

Text 1 Stealing History

<u>5</u> SB p. 68 Getting Started
A.
1. b, d, e

<u>7</u> SB p. 69 Active Previewing
A.
1. Joseph Braude
2. loot Iraqi artifacts
3. the Iraqi National Museum or Iraq
4. August

C.
1. Joseph Braude, some stolen artifacts from Iraq, a Princeton alumnus who smuggled some artifacts from Iraq
2. Joseph Braude smuggled some artifacts out of Iraq and was arrested; A Princeton alumnus was arrested for smuggling some artifacts out of Iraq.

<u>9</u> SB p. 70 Understanding the Text
A.
1. six months under house arrest and two years' probation

2. in a routine customs examination (customs agents at J.F.K. airport found three seals in his suitcase that Braude had not declared)
3. to research an introduction to his new book

B.
1. Iraq, 2
2. U.S., 1
3. U.S., 5
4. U.S., 4
5. U.S., 6
6. Iraq, 3

[11] SB p. 71 Understanding the Topic and Main Idea

1. a Princeton alumnus who stole some Iraqi artifacts
2.
   a. MI
   b. S
   c. G

[13] SB p. 72 Understanding Possessive Adjectives

1.
   a. Braude
   b. Braude
2. Iraq
3.
   a. Braude
   b. the new Iraq

[14] SB p. 72 Understanding Vocabulary in Context—Context Clues

2, 3, 5

Text 2   Recreating an Army

[16] SB p. 73 Getting Started

A.
2. a
3. b, d, e

[18] SB p. 74 Active Previewing

A.
1. Who: a retired marine captain (OR the technical adviser for Alexander)

2. What: a technical adviser on war scenes for films
3. When: 2,400 years ago

C.
1. Dale Dye, how Dale Dye prepared actors for the move Alexander, Dale Dye's work on the movie Alexander
2. Dale Dye is the technical adviser for the movie Alexander; Dale Dye prepared the actors to act like Macedonian soldiers for the movie Alexander; Dale Dye's work on the movie Alexander was to prepare the actors.

[20] SB p. 76 Understanding the Text

A.
1. helps create realistic war environments for movies; trains actors to behave like military men
2. studied ancient Roman scholars
3. three weeks of hard workouts; they went through the conditioning of a Macedonian soldier

B.
1. a
2. b
3. b
4. a
5. c

[22] SB p. 76 Understanding the Topic and Main Idea

A.
1. technical adviser Dale Dye
2.
   a. S
   b. MI
   c. G

B.
1.
   a. T
   b. S
   c. G
2.
   a. G
   b. MI
   c. S

3.
   a. S
   b. G
   c. T
4.
   a. S
   b. G
   c. MI

[25] SB p. 78 Understanding Supporting Details
1. a, b
2. a, c

[27] SB p. 79 Understanding Vocabulary in Context—Collocations
1. c
2. b
3. a
4. c
5. b

Text 3 Ancient Egypt: A Timeline

[32] SB p. 80 Active Previewing
1. approximately 2000 years
2. six
3. the history of Ancient Egypt

[34] SB p. 80 Understanding the Graphics
Old Kingdom, First Intermediate, Middle Kingdom, Second Intermediate, New Kingdom

[35] SB p. 82 Scanning
2. Amarna
3. the Second Intermediate period
4. the Early Dynastic period; 2623–2494 B.C.E.
5. the New Kingdom period: the religious center moved from Thebes to Amarna and Egypt's state religion changed to the cult of Aten; the religious center moved back to Thebes and original religion was restored

Text 4 A Newly Discovered Ancient City

[38] SB p. 82 Getting Started
A.
   2.
      a. a pyramid (Chichén Itzá in Mexico)
      b. Machu Picchu, Peru
      c. an archaeological site (Caral, Peru)

B.
   2, 4, 5

[39] SB p. 83 Active Previewing
C.
1. Caral, an ancient civilization discovered in Peru, an archaeologist who discovered an ancient Peruvian civilization
2. Caral may be one of the oldest known civilizations in the world; An ancient civilization in Peru could be one of the oldest in the world; An archaeologist discovered an ancient Peruvian civilization.

[41] SB p. 86 Understanding the Text
A.
1. Caral might be the oldest city in the Americas and one of the most ancient in the world.
2. a Peruvian archaeologist
3. the Inca

B.
2. Caral could be pre-ceramic (and might predate Olmec settlements by 1,000 years)
3. the reeds were good subjects for radiocarbon dating; original workers must have filled bags with stones from a quarry about a mile away
4. suggest that Caral was a major trade center
5. Caral might have existed so far inland and become an important civilization because of its cotton trade (it grew cotton that fishermen needed for nets)

C.
   2, 5, 1, 4, 3

44 SB p. 86 Understanding the Topic, Main Idea, and Supporting Details

A.

1. the ancient city of Caral
2.
   a. G
   b. S
   c. MI

B.

1.
   a. MI
   b. T
   c. SD

2.
   a. SD
   b. MI
   c. T

3.
   a. MI
   b. T
   c. SD

4. A 30-foot-wide staircase rises from a circular plaza at the foot of the pyramid. There are the remains of an atrium. Thousands of manual laborers and many architects, craftsmen, supervisors, and other managers would have been needed to build the pyramid. A large amphitheater could have held many hundreds of people during civic or religious events.

47 SB p. 87 Understanding Possessive Adjectives

2. Shady
3. the people of Caral
4. Caral's early farmers
5. the people of Caral

48 SB p. 88 Understanding Vocabulary in Context

A.

1. a
2. b
3. a

B.

1. a
2. c
3. c
4. b
5. b

CHAPTER 5 STRANGE PHENOMENA

3 SB p. 91 Chapter Introduction

2.
   a. a UFO or flying saucer
   b. a ghost
   c. a fortune teller
   d. a palm reader

Text 1 Psychic or Not?

5 SB p. 92 Getting Started

A.

2, 5, 6

6 SB p. 92 Active Previewing

C.

1. psychics; psychic detectives
2. a psychic uses her abilities to help find missing people

8 SB p. 94 Understanding the Text

A.

1. she uses her psychic abilities
2. They believe she has special psychic powers. (Police departments use psychics; 35% of urban police departments have used a psychic at one time or another.)
3. He doesn't believe she has special psychic powers. (Psychics are really just highly imaginative and emotional people who make more guesses but are no more successful than anyone else.)

B.

1. Keaton
2. Nickell
3. Keaton
4. Nickell
5. Nickell

10 SB p. 95 Understanding the Topic, Main Idea, and Supporting Details

A.
1. how psychic Annette Martin helps find missing people
2. Psychic Annette Martin uses her abilities to help police departments locate missing people.

B.
1. psychic Annette Martin
   a. SD
   b. MI
2. how Martin finds missing people
   a. MI
   b. SD
3. the missing murder suspect
   a. MI
   b. SD

12 SB p. 95 Understanding Vocabulary in Context—Idioms

1. c
2. b
3. a
4. a
5. c

14 SB p. 96 Reading Critically—Fact and Opinion

1. O
2. O
3. F
4. F
5. O

Text 2   New York Taste

19 SB p. 97 Active Previewing

A.
1. synesthetes
2. synesthesia
3. the brain
4. early 1900's, by 1910

C.
1. synesthesia; synesthetes, a sixth sense
2. Synesthesia is a rare brain condition in which some of the senses are joined together.

21 SB p. 99 Understanding the Text

A.
1. a rare brain condition in which some of the senses are joined together, creating almost literally a sixth sense
2. music is seen and felt; words have flavors, flavors have colors, letters have colors
3. no

B.
1, 3, 4

23 SB p. 100 Understanding the Topic, Main Idea, and Supporting Details

A.
1. synesthesia
2. Synesthesia is a rare brain condition in which some of the senses are joined together.

B.
1. synesthesia
2.
   c. MI
3. words have flavors; flavors have color
4. synasthetes' feeling of isolation
5.
   a. MI
6. many are afraid of being ridiculed; many keep their condition to themselves
7. McAllister's brain scan
8.
   b. MI
9. there was activity in the visual area of his brain even though he was only listening to music

27 SB p. 101 Understanding Vocabulary in Context—Contrasts

1. disagree
2. belong with the rest of the world
3. normal

28 SB p. 101 Reading Critically—Fact and Opinion

2. O
3. F
4. O
5. O

Text 3 Believe It or Not

31 SB p. 102 Getting Started
1. c
2. a
3. d
4. e
5. b

32 SB p. 103 Active Previewing
1. Belief in Paranormal Phenomena
2. 1990, 1996, 2001, 2005
3. belief in paranormal phenomena

33 SB p. 104 Scanning
1. 2001
2. psychic or spiritual healing power of the human mind to heal the body
3. extrasensory perception
4. psychic or spiritual healing power of the human mind to heal the body
5. 30%

34 SB p. 104 Understanding the Graphics
2. 2001, 1990, 2005
3. 2001, 2005, 1996, 1990
4. 2001, 1990, 1996, 2005
5. 2005, 2001, 1990

Text 4 Coincidence or Random Chance

39 SB p. 105 Active Previewing
C.
1. the power of coincidence; coincidence
2. Believers and skeptics have different ideas about coincidence; Believers and skeptics are fascinated by coincidence.

41 SB p. 109 Understanding the Text
A.
1. coincidence is chance
2. coincidence is the purposeful occurrence of two seemingly unrelated events
3. comets were cosmic messages of some kind
4. coincidence is not as unlikely as one might believe

5. events that have a worldwide impact are able to focus people's consciousness

B.
1. F "does not have special meaning"
2. F "just one comet"
3. T
4. T
5. F "the day of the attacks"

44 SB p. 110 Understanding the Topic, Main Idea, and Supporting Details
A.
1. what skeptics and believers think about coincidence
2.
   a. MI

B.
1. comets as cosmic messages
2.
   b. MI
3. in England in 1066, a comet appeared just before the Battle of Hastings was fought over the throne; a comet appeared before the Great Plague of 1665; a comet appeared in 1532 before Francisco Pizarro arrived in South America to conquer the Incan Indians in South America
4. the likelihood of coincidence
5.
   b. MI
6. each person has plenty of opportunity to experience coincidences in his life
7. what Radin believes about significant events
8.
   a. MI
9. On Sept. 11, 2001, before the attacks, the generators were noisy; the next day, there was a drop; On March 11, 2004, after the attacks, it was noisy; the next day it was quiet.

48 SB p. 111 Understanding Vocabulary in Context—Synonyms
2. awareness
3. the minds of everyone on the planet
4. sharp increase
5. current accepted theory

49 SB p. 112 Reading Critically—Fact and Opinion

2. O
3. O
4. F
5. F

CHAPTER 6   RETHINKING BUSINESS

3 SB p. 115 Chapter Introduction

2.
   a. children selling their products
   b. a socially responsible business activity
   c. pollution

Text 1   The Future of Business

7 SB p. 117 Active Previewing

A.
1. a group of young entrepreneurs
2. They pitched business ideas to local professionals.
3. recently
4. Baton Rouge

C.
1. young entrepreneurs; an opportunity for young entrepreneurs
2. Young entrepreneurs in Baton Rouge had the opportunity to pitch their business ideas to local professionals; Young entrepreneurs are learning about business from professionals.

9 SB p. 119 Understanding the Text

A.
1. to teach young children about business
2. participants must be good students and their parents or guardians must sign a contract committing the students for three years
3. local business professionals

B.
2. feedback on writing style and format of business plans
3. business style and etiquette
4. coming up with their own brands and slogans
5. "dress for success" tips

11 SB p. 119 Understanding the Topic and Main Idea

1. how the YES program teaches children about business
2. The YES program teaches children about business by pairing the children up with local business professionals.

12 SB p. 120 Understanding Pronouns and Possessive Adjectives

1.
   b. a group of young entrepreneurs
2.
   a. Tommy Fronseca
   b. the students
   c. successful adults
3.
   a. the participants
   b. Dean Loyd
   c. Charlsey Loyd

14 SB p. 121 Reading Critically—Facts, Opinions, and Inferences

A.
1. c
2. b
3. a

B.
2. F
3. O
4. I
5. F

Text 2   Are Businesses Out of Control?

21 SB p. 123 Active Previewing

C.
1. corporate responsibility, corporations and reform
2. Laws should be changed to make corporations act more responsibly; Corporations should act more responsibly.

23 SB p. 126 Understanding the Text

A.
1. They are like psychopaths.
2. They are decent/responsible people.

3. changing the laws that create/control corporations

B.
1, 2, 4, 7

25 SB p. 126 Understanding the Topic, Main Idea, and Supporting Details

A.
1. corporate responsibility; corporate irresponsibility
2. Laws should be changed so that corporations are required to act more responsibly.

B.
1. corporations' pursuit of profit
2.
   b. MI
3. they hurt the environment; they violate human rights and the dignity of employees; they endanger public health and safety and the welfare of communities
4. the people who run corporations
5.
   a. MI
6. they care about the environment and other people; corporate abuse is not due to flaws in their character
7. state laws that create corporations
8. State laws that create corporations encourage behavior that managers and shareholders don't approve of in their private lives.
9. they encourage managers to behave as if shareholders are psychopaths; they allow managers to excuse themselves from the damage they do

30 SB p. 128 Understanding Reflexive Pronouns

1. the underlying cause
2. the environment
3. the citizens (in whose name the corporate laws were enacted)
4. corporate managers
5. corporations

31 SB p. 128 Understanding Vocabulary in Context—Synonyms

1. defects

2. people who own stock in a company
3. to support
4. selfish
5. to change

32 SB p. 129 Reading Critically—Facts, Opinions, and Inferences

2. O
3. F
4. I
5. O

Text 3 The Cycle of Motivation

37 SB p. 130 Active Previewing

1. Demotivation and Motivation
2. how feedback affects motivation

38 SB p. 131 Understanding the Graphics

2. hesitant attempts
3. hesitant attempts
4. strong results
5. confidence

39 SB p. 131 Reading Critically—Facts, Opinions, and Inferences

2. I
3. F
4. I
5. O

Text 4 When Beauty Meets Business

42 SB p. 132 Getting Started

A.
2. a, b, d, f, g

44 SB p. 133 Active Previewing

C.
1. Anita Roddick; Anita Roddick and the Body Shop
2. Anita Roddick used creativity to overcome challenges and to create her company, the Body Shop.

46 SB p. 135 Understanding the Text

A.
1. the founder of the Body Shop
2. it is a powerfully effective vehicle for social and environmental awareness and change
3. naturally based cosmetics
4. she was looking for a way to feed herself and her two children
5. their willingness to recognize what wasn't working and quickly identify a new way to approach a problem

B.
1. Roddick used products no one had heard of before.
2. She never advertised.
3. She put ideals before profit.
4. She cared about the environment.
5. She made cruelty-free products.

48 SB p. 136 Understanding the Topic, Main Idea, and Supporting Details

A.
1. Anita Roddick and the Body Shop
2. Anita Roddick has used creativity and vision to create a successful and responsible cosmetics company, the Body Shop.

B.
1. the results of Anita's irreverence
2.
   c. MI
3. there are more than 1,500 stores around the world; The Body Shop is worth over $500 million; it has influenced products and marketing of all major competitors; it is a powerfully effective vehicle for social and environmental change
4. how Anita started her company (with no finances)
5. Anita started her company with almost no finances.
6. bottled cosmetics in plastic containers; encouraged customers to bring containers back for refills; hand-printed labels
7. Anita's ideals in business
8. Anita put her ideals before profit in her company.
9. Anita wanted to change the entire face of business; she believes the human spirit plays

a big role in business; believes business can be a human enterprise that people feel good about

52 SB p. 137 Understanding Pronouns and Possessive Adjectives

1.
   b. most entrepreneurs
   c. Anita
   d. Anita
2.
   a. Anita
   b. Anita
   c. young female consumers
3.
   a. Anita
   b. labels
   c. the cosmetics

53 SB p. 138 Understanding Vocabulary in Context—Collocations

1. e
2. b
3. c
4. a
5. d

54 SB p. 138 Reading Critically—Making Inferences

2. imaginative: Roddick hand-printed labels; she got customers around one mall to write letters so the mall would rent her a space.
3. strong-willed: kept the name "The Body Shop" even though local funeral parlors wanted her to change it; she didn't advertise for the opening of The Body Shop in the U.S. even though people told her it was suicide.
4. caring: Roddick decided her shops would be a spark for change; she put ideals ahead of profit; her business creates work for people in underdeveloped countries.
5. flexible: Roddick used inexpensive containers and hand-printed labels because she couldn't afford more; her willingness to approach problems in a new way.

Text 1 The Mediterranean Diet

8 SB p. 143 Active Previewing

A.

1. Mediterranean people
2. eating a Mediterranean diet
3. France, Italy, Greece, Spain; Mediterranean countries

C.

1. the Mediterranean diet, eating healthfully, good nutrition
2. The Mediterranean diet may help people live longer; Eating healthfully is important for a long life.

10 SB p. 145 Understanding the Text

A.

1. He thought is was a good diet. (He was its best advertisement.)
2. a diet that contains mostly fruits and vegetables and little dairy (other details: a lot of fish, but little meat; little alcohol; plant-based fats/oils).
3. that the Mediterranean diet was linked to a longer life

B.

2. eat a lot of fish but little meat
3. drink little alcohol
4. eat mostly plant-based oils (that haven't been too refined)

12 SB p. 145 Understanding the Topic and Main Idea

1. the Mediterranean diet; the health benefits of a Mediterranean diet
2. The Mediterranean diet may help people live longer.

14 SB p. 146 Understanding Demonstrative Pronouns

1. people (in nine European countries)
2. "olive oil good, saturated fats bad"
3. that red wine offers health advantages over other forms of alcohol

15 SB p. 146 Understanding Vocabulary in Context—Context Clues

1. c
2. a
3. b

16 SB p. 147 Reading Critically—Facts, Opinions, and Inferences

2. O
3. I
4. I
5. F

Text 2 The Joy of Soy

19 SB p. 148 Getting Started

A.

1. a, b, d, f, h, j

B.

heart disease—get more exercise and eat more healthfully, etc.
osteoporosis—maintain bone density by eating foods rich in calcium, like soy.

22 SB p. 149 Skimming

A.

1. eat soy products
2. soy beans, tofu, soy milk
3. heart disease, high cholesterol, osteoporosis, cancer
4. 25
5. China and Japan

C.

1. eating soy, eating soy to improve health the benefits of soy
2. Eating soy may improve our health; Studies show that eating soy is good for health.

25 SB p. 152 Understanding the Text

A.

1. a plant food (that is high in protein)
2. good
3. at most supermarkets

B.

2. Soy stabilizes the hormone estrogen

3. Soy reduces cholesterol and protects against heart disease
4. Soy may protect against osteoporosis
5. Soy may protect against cancer or revert cancer cells to normal

26 SB p. 152 Understanding the Topic, Main Idea, and Supporting Details

A.
1. the benefits of eating soy
2. Eating soy has many health benefits.

B.
1. (the benefits of) isoflavones
2. Many of the health benefits of soy come from its isoflavones.
3. they stabilize estrogen; they adjust the levels when they are too high or too low
4. soy's ability to reduce cholesterol and protect against heart disease
5. Studies have shown that soy can reduce cholesterol and protect against heart disease.
6. 38 studies in New England Journal of Medicine: soy lowers total levels of cholesterol by 10% and bad cholesterol by 13%; FDA suggests eating 25 grams of soy per day; American Heart Association recommends soy as part of a heart-healthy diet.
7. soy's ability to protect against osteoporosis
8. Studies show that soy may help protect against osteoporosis.
9. American Journal of Clinical Nutrition: postmenopausal women who eat 40 grams of soy increase bone density; University of Iowa study: women who consume soy maintain bone density; Mark Messina at Loma Linda University: if you subsitute soy for animal protein, you'll lose less calcium.

30 SB p. 153 Understanding Demonstrative Pronouns
2. that soy reduces cholesterol and protects against heart disease
3. women
4. free radicals
5. a wide variety of soy foods; soy nuts, snack bars, and instant shakes

32 SB p. 154 Understanding Vocabulary in Context

A.
1. adjust
2. showed
3. at risk

B.
1. a
2. c
3. c
4. a
5. b

34 SB p. 154 Reading Critically—Facts, Opinions, and Inferences
2. F
3. I
4. O
5. I

Text 3 Pyramids of Health

39 SB p. 155 Active Previewing
1. the Mediterranean and Asia
2. traditional diets (from these regions)

40 SB p. 156 Understanding the Graphics
1. meat
2. to eat them weekly
3. breads, rice, noodles, pasta, etc.

40 SB p. 156 Reading Critically—Facts, Opinions, and Inferences
2. I
3. F
4. O
5. I

Text 4 Chili Peppers and Globalization

45 SB p. 157 Skimming

A.
1. a fruit
2. the chili pepper
3. Middle and South America

4. Thailand, the United States, Mexico, the Middle East, North Africa, Southern India, China, Korea, Singapore, Malaysia, Indonesia, Hawaii
5. they offer a full day's supply of beta-carotene, two times' the daily allowance of Vitamin C; they control pain; they reduce pain associated with arthritis, diabetes, muscle and joint problems, cluster headaches, phantom limbs, and post-surgical scars; they alleviate the symptoms of the common cold; they increase metabolism; they lower bad cholesterol; they can prevent formation of blood clots

C.

1. the chili pepper, chili peppers around the world
2. Chili peppers are eaten/enjoyed in cuisines around the world and also have some medical benefits, Chili peppers are eaten by many cultures around the world.

48 SB p. 161 Understanding the Text

A.

1. They love them.
2. capsaicin
3. in many countries around the world
4. they reduce pain associated with arthritis, diabetes, muscle and joint problems, cluster headaches, phantom limbs; Mayo Clinic: they reduce pain of post-surgical scars; Max Planck Institute: they can prevent formation of blood clots
5. Humans get pleasure out of fear.

B.

2. they can alleviate symptoms by breaking up congestion
3. they can increase the metabolic rate
4. they can reduce bad cholesterol
5. they can prevent their formation

50 SB p. 162 Understanding the Topic, Main Idea, and Supporting Details

A.

1. chili peppers around the world

2. Chili peppers are eaten/enjoyed in cuisines around the world and may also have many medical benefits.

B.

1. chili peppers from a medical perspective
2. Chili peppers are attracting attention from a medical perspective.
3. a single pepper provides a full day's supply of beta-carotene; a single pepper provides twice the daily allowance of Vitamin C; capsaicin controls pain and makes us feel better
4. capsaicin's ability to reduce pain
5. Studies suggest that capsaicin can reduce different kinds of pain.
6. reduces pain associated with arthritis, diabetes, muscle and joint problems, cluster headaches, and phantom limbs; reduces pain from post-surgical scars; people with chronic pain are now being advised to eat spicy food
7. other medical advantages of chili peppers
8. Chili peppers possess other medical advantages.
9. they alleviate symptoms of the common cold; a capsaicin nose spray is not being considered for headaches and migraines; chili peppers increase the metabolism; they lower bad cholesterol; they prevent the formation of blood clots

54 SB p. 163 Understanding Demonstrative Pronouns

2. five separate chemical components
3. Tabasco sauce
4. the messages sent to your brain
5. som tam

55 SB p. 163 Understanding Vocabulary in Context

A.

1. to convey
2. to be credited with
3. to be stripped

B.

1. d
2. c
3. e

4. a
5. b

56 **SB p. 164 Reading Critically—Facts, Opinions, and Inferences**

    2. I
    3. O
    4. I
    5. F

CHAPTER 8   ETHICS IN SCIENCE

Text 1   Should Animals Have Rights?

7 **SB p. 168 Getting Started**

B.
    1. All are.

8 **SB p. 169 Active Previewing**

A.
    1. Rutgers University and PETA
    2. animal testing
    3. recently
    4. Rutgers University

C.
    1. animal testing at Rutgers University, animal testing, PETA's concerns about animal testing at Rutgers University
    2. Animal testing at Rutgers University has become a problem for PETA; PETA has concerns about animal testing at Rutgers University.

11 **SB p. 171 Understanding the Text**

A.
    1. animal testing
    2. a group that believes in the ethical treatment of animals
    3. that the animal testing practices could be cruel

B.
    1. Animal testing gives valuable results.
    2. Animal testing is not the only way to conduct research.
    3. Ensures that the animals are treated properly.

12 **SB p. 171 Understanding the Topic and Main Idea**

    1. PETA's concerns about animal testing at Rutgers University
    2. PETA is concerned about whether animal testing at Rutgers University is ethical.

13 **SB p. 172 Understanding Pronouns**

    2. the committee
    3. the policy
    4. Katz
    5. an experiment

14 **SB p. 172 Understanding Vocabulary in Context**

A.
    2. strictly
    3. to violate

B.
    2. horses and mules
    3. cows and oxen

15 **SB p. 172 Reading Critically—Facts, Opinions, and Inferences**

    2. F
    3. I
    4. I
    5. O

Text 2   Part Animal, Part Human?

18 **SB p. 173 Getting Started**

A.
    1. b
    2. liger (lion/tiger), zorse (zebra/horse), wolphin (whale/dolphin)

20 **SB p. 173 Active Previewing**

C.
    1. animal-human hybrids, chimera, animal-human hybrids in medical research, ethical problems with animal-human hybrids
    2. Animal-human hybrids have been developed for the sake of research in medicine; Chimera are animal-human hybrids that have been developed for medical research; There are

some ethical issues regarding the creation of animal-human hybrids for research in medicine.

22 SB p. 176 Understanding the Text

A.
1. creatures that are part animal, part human
2. for better treatments in medicine
3. the ethics involved in combining humans with another species

B.
2. has happened already
3. has not happened
4. has happened already
5. has not happened

24 SB p. 177 Understanding the Topic and Main Idea

1. ethical concerns with animal-human hybrids in medical research
2. There are some ethical concerns about animal-human hybrids that have been developed for the sake of research in medicine.

25 SB p. 177 Understanding Demonstrative Pronouns

2. cross animals with another species
3. to produce a child whose parents are a pair of mice
4. people putting their own moral beliefs in the way of this kind of science
5. (creating) mice that have 100 percent human brains

26 SB p. 177 Understanding Vocabulary in Context

A.
2. to cut apart
3. signs

B.
2. to prohibit
3. (overall) structure

27 SB p. 178 Reading Critically—Facts, Opinions, and Inferences

2. O
3. I
4. F
5. O

Text 3 Public Opinion on Gene Therapy

31 SB p. 179 Active Previewing

1. eliminating deafness or blindness; eliminating disease; improving intelligence; altering height and weight
2. gene therapy

32 SB p. 180 Scanning

1. 2.36
2. 4.03
3. altering height and weight
4. 23%
5. to alter height and weight

Text 4 Savior Siblings, Designer Babies

36 SB p. 181 Getting Started

A.
2. a, b, e, f, g

38 SB p. 181 Skimming

A.
1. they wanted to have a baby by in vitro fertilization
2. permanent changes to the human race
3. two

C.
1. genetic research, genetic research for medical advances, ethical issues of genetic research
2. There are some ethical issues regarding genetic research that is currently being done; New genetic research may change medicine and perhaps even the human race forever.

41 SB p. 185 Understanding the Text

A.

1. They both needed to have a savior sibling in order to save the life of an existing child through gene therapy.
2. a child who is conceived to save the life of his brother or sister by giving him or her healthy genes
3. to deliver genetic treatments safely
4. pre-programmed genetic treatments delivered through an artificial chromosome
5. There could be two different species.

44 SB p. 186 Understanding the Topic, Main Idea, and Supporting Details

A.

1. ethical issues of genetic research
2. New genetic research may change medicine and perhaps even the human race forever.

B.

1. Topic: the Hashmi's desire to have a baby by in vitro fertilization
2. The Hashmis desired to have a baby by in vitro fertilization to create a savior sibling for their son.
3. they wanted the baby to be free of genetic disease; they wanted it to be tested so it would match the tissue of the son who had a genetic disorder
4. a savior sibling
5. A savior sibling is a child who is conceived in order to save the life of a brother or sister.
6. the children are tested when they are still embryos to ensure that they are free from genetic disorders
7. engineering the human gene pool
8. Scientists believe they may be able to engineer the human gene pool for the first time.
9. the modifications would have a permanent effect on the human species; these modifications are called "germline" gene therapy; future generations would be changed forever; today's "designer babies" are low-tech in comparison

48 SB p. 186 Understanding Pronouns and Possessive Adjectives

1.
   b. Raj and Shashana Hashmi
   c. the baby
   d. the baby
   e. Raj and Shashana Hashmi
2.
   a. standard gene therapy
   b. Jesse Gelsinger
   c. Jesse Gelsinger
   d. Jesse Gelsinger
3.
   a. that HACs are safer than other ways of introducing foreign genes into the body
   b. the DNA of the artificial chromosomes
   c. HACs
   d. "it insertion"

51 SB p. 187 Understanding Vocabulary in Context

A.

2. deadly
3. to change or modify
4. copy
5. extreme
6. to get rid of
7. a number
8. make children

B.

2. complexities
3. to be protected